Little Chapels, Grateful Hearts

Fr. Edward Looney
Illustrated by Ayan Mansoori

Little Chapels, Grateful Hearts

Written by: Fr. Edward Looney
Illustrated by: Ayan Mansoori

First Edition: 2023
ISBN: 979-8-9884033-2-6
No part of this book may be reproduced or reprinted without the permission of the author.

Dedication

In gratitude to the Belgian Communities I
served as pastor from 2017-2023.
I write this story with the hope that the
customs and traditions of the Belgians might
continue for generations to come.

Catholic Devotion in Belgium

The country of Belgium did not exist until 1830. But the land we know as Belgium has been around for several centuries and had many holy priests and monks who shared the Catholic faith. One of them was St. Amandus who lived in the 600s. He was a monk and built monasteries throughout Belgium which were centers of prayer and teaching. Other popular saints who helped include St. Eligius, St. Willibrord, St. Lambert, and St. Hubert. St. Hubert is very popular because he is the patron saint of hunters. All these people were bishops and helped establish the Catholic faith in Belgium.

As the years went by, people began to express their love of Jesus, Mary, and the saints in different ways. All throughout Belgium there were trees that had statues of Jesus, Mary, or the saints. People would walk by these trees and say a prayer or would visit in a time of need. Sometimes the people would walk around the tree three times while saying prayers for a sick family member.

One time a shepherd boy noticed a statue of Mary on the ground and wanted to take it home. But when he picked it up, he couldn't move. It was like he was stuck in the mud. Lots of people looked for him when he didn't come home. When he was found, the statue was removed from his hands and put back in the tree. No longer was he frozen in time, but now could move around and go back home to share the crazy story. Many people believed this was a sign that a shrine should be built to Mary in that location. The church was built in the 1600s and people still visit it today.

The Belgians Come to America

Many of the people who lived in Belgium decided to leave their home country in the 1850s and decided to come to America. They thought they might have a better life in America and would find happiness and wealth. They also expected the weather to be better and they could work the land as farmers. A lot of Belgian people came to Wisconsin. They formed a settlement and began to build Belgian communities in Northeast Wisconsin. These Wisconsin towns would become known with names from cities in Belgium like Brussels, Namur, and Duval.

The Belgians Build Roadside Chapels

When the Belgians came to America, they brought their past experiences of life with them. They started to do many of the same things they did in Belgium in their new land. The practice of placing statues in trees in Belgium became little chapels along the side of the road. These chapels can be seen when you visit the country of Belgium today. But you can also see similar chapels in Wisconsin. Some of the immigrants who lived here built chapels too. Maybe you've seen these little buildings along the road when you are on the way to school or to grandma's house.

Some chapels were built as a reminder of how God heard their prayers. They prayed and were healed. With grateful hearts they built a chapel so other people could pray to God too. Others built chapels because they wanted a peaceful place to pray. Some chapels were built to remember a church that closed.

Some chapels are simple. Others are very pretty. Some are easy to find. Others are hidden. Some are old. Others are new. They are dedicated to Jesus, Mary, and some popular saints like St. Jude or St. Anthony or unknown saints like St. Roch or St. Donat. Each chapel has a story. Let's learn about a few of them.

Mr. Joe Can See Again

Mr. Joe was a hard-working man, husband, and father. He went to work every day so he could feed and clothe his family.

He built buildings with stone and concrete and sometimes had to use dangerous chemicals that could hurt his body if he wasn't careful.

One day at work he had an accident. Some lye got on his face and in his eye. His eye burnt and his face hurt. He didn't think he would ever see again.

When he prayed that night with his wife and kids, he prayed to St. Odile, the patron saint of eye problems. He asked her to beg God to restore his eyesight and he would build a roadside chapel to honor God similar to those in Belgium.

The next morning Mr. Joe woke up and, to his surprise, he could see out of his eye. He knew what he had to do. He started building St. Odile's Chapel immediately.

That chapel was built in 1870. Mr. Joe's relatives have continued to take care of the chapel for many decades now. His memory and what God did for him has never been forgotten. Every time a person visits his chapel, they are reminded of the miracle of his eyesight.

Mr. Pirlot Didn't Drown

It is hard to imagine what life was like many years ago. For years, many people did not have electricity. That means there were no lights and no refrigerators. How would a person keep their food cold? They would cut blocks of ice out of the frozen water and make an icebox in their home.

Mr. Pirlot went to the bay and began cutting his ice to bring home. He fell on the ice and slipped into the water. He thought he might drown because he didn't know how he would get back on the ice. Suddenly he felt someone pulling him up. He was rescued from the water but when he looked around, there was nobody there. Could it have been his Guardian Angel or the Blessed Mother whose scapular he wore and rosary he prayed? He believed it to be Mary because he prayed a Hail Mary while he was drowning, thinking of the hour of his death.

On Mr. Pirlot's journey home with the ice for his icebox, he saw a roadside chapel. He stopped inside and said a prayer of thanksgiving. As he looked at the statue of Mary in the chapel, he said to her, "I will build you a chapel too." He built it by his home and every time he went to cut ice on the bay, he would say a prayer asking Mary to protect him and bring him back home to his family. His chapel reminded him of the day he almost drowned and how grateful he was to be alive.

Fr. Ed Needs a Place to Pray

It was the dream of every Catholic family to have a son become a priest or a daughter to become a religious sister. Joe and Odile Le Mieux's dream came true when their son Edward entered the seminary and studied for the priesthood. He was ordained a priest on June 11, 1920, and served many parishes in the Diocese of Green Bay.

When Fr. Ed visited his mom and dad on his day off, he needed a place to pray quietly. The house was loud and busy. A chapel would be quiet and still. Odile asked her husband and brother if they would build her a chapel and then her son could pray there too. They both agreed and started building the little house of prayer.

Odile was so happy when they finished the chapel. She would visit almost daily and say her prayers because she couldn't visit the parish church as often anymore on account of her advanced age and poor health.

Every June, Odile's family would gather in the chapel and together they would pray the rosary and the novena to St. Anthony, the patron of the chapel. St. Anthony is a special patron who helps people find lost objects. St. Anthony is also known for his beautiful homilies that touched many people's hearts. In this chapel, Fr. Ed would also be inspired in the words he would say at Mass each Sunday.

Today, the St. Anthony Chapel in the Woods is located along a nature trail at University of Wisconsin-Green Bay. It is still visited by the family of Fr. Ed and many other people stop by to say a quick prayer while they enjoy the beauty of God's creation.

When Someone Has Cancer

People get sick. Sometimes their sickness does not go away as quickly as a cold but stays with them for a long time. Some people will get sicker each day and it is hard to see them that way. This happens when someone has cancer. People try to get better from cancer with the help of doctors and medicines. Their treatment sometimes makes them sick for a few days at a time and they might even look different.

One of the things you can do is pray for people with cancer. There is a special saint who is known to pray for those with cancer. His name is St. Peregrine. He also had cancer and knows what people with cancer are experiencing which means he can pray better for them.

There is a chapel in the back of St. Hubert Church's parking lot in Rosiere. You must walk along a little path to get to the chapel. This is one of the most visited chapels because so many people have cancer. A visitor can light a candle, write down someone's name, and bow their head in prayer asking for St. Peregrine's powerful prayers before the throne of God.

Bonnie Always Wanted a Chapel

When Bonnie was a young girl, her parents and grandparents would visit many of the roadside chapels. Her mom and dad said, "This is what we do, we are Belgians." In these chapels, she would pray the Our Father and Hail Mary.

As Bonnie grew up and got married, she and her husband started a family. Bonnie would take her children to see the chapels, just like her parents did for her. And like her, they would pray the prayers they learned.

It was always Bonnie's dream to have a chapel at her house. She didn't know when that would happen.

Suddenly, Bonnie was sick with cancer and didn't know how much longer she had. She told her husband, "Now is the time to build the chapel."

Many people build the chapels because they were healed. Bonnie built hers with the hope she would be healed.

Bonnie needed surgery and many people prayed for her. Lots of people do not get better from the cancer she had. But she did. Her cancer is gone and now she spends time with her grandkids in her chapel.

She called her chapel, Our Lady of Peace, because when she prayed there, she experienced feelings of peace.

Dr. Doug Prays Everyday

Dr. Doug was an older gentleman who loved Jesus and his Catholic faith.

He went to a shrine of Mary often to go confession and attend Mass and receive Holy Communion.

He traveled throughout the world to visit places where Mary appeared and to see the sites of popular saints like Padre Pio.

Dr. Doug read a lot of books and learned a lot about different saints and devotions of the Catholic faith.

He learned about St. Bridget of Sweden who saw visions of Jesus and his passion. Because she loved Jesus, she wrote 15 prayers about the passion of Jesus.

Many people throughout the world prayed these prayers including Dr. Doug.

As Dr. Doug aged, he wanted a place close to home to pray. He knew about the roadside chapels and decided to build one in his yard.

He put an altar, a crucifix, statues, and a stained-glass window in the chapel. If you visited his house and he didn't answer the door, you would look in the chapel and see if he was there. Normally he would be, and you would see him with a prayer book or a rosary in his hand as he talked to God and prayed for others.

The roadside chapels might be visited by a person passing by for just a few minutes or others like Dr. Doug who had a habit of daily prayer.

Grandma Char Prays with Her Grandkids

Grandma Char met her husband many years ago and married him. They built their home and formed a family. They watched their children grow up so quickly and made many memories with them. Their two sons and daughter found their spouses and began forming a family of their own. Now seven little boys and girls call Char 'grandma'.

One year, Grandma Char went on a trip of a lifetime to visit the places where Jesus was born and died in the Holy Land. During that trip she was worried for her children who were preparing to have babies. She prayed at special sites like the Church of the Visitation or the Milk Grotto asking that her grandchildren would be healthy.

Grandma Char was able to hold her newborn grandbaby in her arms and felt the same joy and thankfulness of Mary and Elizabeth from the Visitation. When Mary visited Elizabeth, she sang a hymn of praise to God called the Magnificat. Grandma Char wanted to sing her own song of praise and thanks to God. She thought a chapel was a good idea.

Grandpa built the chapel in a month, and they dedicated it to Mary's Visitation. Grandma Char hopes that people will pray for healthy babies and fertility when they visit her chapel. But most importantly, she is able to pray now with the grandchildren for whom she prayed many years ago. Every visit with Grandma Char includes a grateful prayer with her little people in her little chapel.

St. Martin's Church Closes

Once upon a time every little community had its own church. There were enough priests to staff them and enough people going to Mass to need them.

As the years went by and people bought cars, it was much easier to travel to church on Sunday. It cost a lot of money to keep a church open. Sometimes a smaller church had to be closed.

Some churches closed because there was a fire and the church suffered lots of damage. In other cases, the church was getting old and cost too much to repair. Some churches closed just because they didn't have enough money.

The little town of Tonet once had a church called St. Martin's Church. It was built in the 1870s and served the Flemish Belgians. A few miles down the road was St. Joseph Church which served the Walloon Belgians.

There was a family that went to Church at St. Martin's, and they had a chapel on their farm. Their chapel was dedicated to praying for people who served in the military during World War I. People gathered to pray for their safety.

When the family could no longer take care of the cemetery, they asked the priest at St. Martin's if the chapel could be in the cemetery. Father thought this was a wonderful idea. During special times of the year, people could process from the church after Mass to the chapel for additional prayers. This could happen on days like Corpus Christi.

In 1992, St. Martin's Church was closed. They celebrated their last Mass together as a community. The next Sunday, people had to go to one of the other churches in a nearby town. After the church closed, a few items from the church, like a statue of St. Martin was placed in the chapel. For the people who went to Mass in Tonet, the roadside chapel became a reminder of their life at St. Martin's.

Other chapels also remember a closed parish like St. Odile's in Thiry Daems and Our Lady of the Snows in Namur. The chapels keep alive the memory of a church that no longer is there. People prayed for many years in those churches and now they can say their prayers in a smaller chapel.

It's Time to Visit the Chapels

The people that live in Northeast Wisconsin have a strong faith and are not afraid to share it. Now you know the story of several chapels but there are many more to learn about and see. There are more than 30 chapels all throughout Brown, Kewaunee, and Door County. Your parents can find a list at the Belgian Heritage Center or by looking for "Belgian Roadside Chapels of Northeastern Wisconsin" on Facebook and your journey to visit the chapels with them can begin.

When you visit, be sure to look around and see how many saints you know and what else you can find. But most importantly, remember when you visit these little chapels, you should have a grateful and prayerful heart. Pray to God and ask the saints to pray for you. Little chapels can be visited by little people with grateful hearts!

About the Author

Fr. Edward Looney was ordained a priest in 2015 and serves as a pastor in the Diocese of Green Bay. He holds a License in Sacred Theology from the University of St. Mary of the Lake and currently serves as the president of the Mariological Society of America. He is an author of popular Marian devotionals for adults including *A Heart Like Mary's, A Rosary Litany, A Lenten Journey with Mother Mary* and *How They Love Mary* and for children he has also authored *Father Looney's Christmas Stories* and *The Story of Sister Adele and Our Lady of Champion.* Fr. Looney directed and hosted the award-winning documentary *Faith Along the Road* about the Roadside Chapels. You can find the documentary on YouTube.